Be Your Own Leader
Learn The Process of Winning at Life

By Paul Scahig

Table of Contents

Introduction

Chapter 1: What Does it mean to lead Your Own life

Chapter 2: Are You Leading your own Life

Chapter 3: The Benefits of Leading Your Own Life

Chapter 4: What Happens if You're Not Leading Your Own Life

Chapter 5: Checking Your ego at the Door

Chapter 6: Committing to Goals

Chapter 7: Ways to Become a Better Personal Leader

Chapter 8: Why you should Question Everything

Chapter 9: How to Appreciate the Good as a Leader

Chapter 10: How to Become Less Pessimistic

Chapter 11: How to Propel Yourself Forward to a Better life

Chapter 12: Learning from Mistakes and Pushing Forward

Conclusion

Introduction

How does life make you feel do you wake up every morning ready to live the best life that you can? Or do you wake up groaning in displeasure at the fact that you're going to have to continue doing the same thing every single day?

If you're feeling the latter, there is a chance that you aren't leading your own life? This is something that everyone gets all caught up in, and it actually can be quite stressful if you aren't leading your own life. If you're not being a leader to yourself, you actually are creating a detrimental situation, and all those goals that you have will get washed away with each and every single day.

If you aren't being your own leader, you can say goodbye to many things, including your own goals, your own happiness, and even feeling good about the world. It's rough out there, but if you are able to work as a leader in your own life, you'll feel even better than you have before.

So, what does it mean to live your own life? How in the world do you do it? Well, you're going to find out, and this book will give you the full lowdown on how to become the leader that you want to be, and why it is important to do so. Being the leader of your own life is so important, and this book will tell you why that is, and the benefits you can reap from doing so.

Chapter 1: What Does it mean to lead Your Own life

The first hurdle you'll reach, is what it means to live your own life? How in the world do you do it? What are the exact mechanisms behind it? Well, you're about to find out, and you'll learn from here just what it takes to lead your own life, and why it is important to do this sort of thing.

What is it?

You've heard of leadership many times. All throughout our lives, we're encouraged by society to be better leaders, to take the torch and run with it. We don't always need to be followers, but instead, we have to take the initiative on various elements of life.

For example, let's take your life. Maybe you have a business that you're running. Let's not go personal. Now look at yourself. When it comes to leading the business, you have to take control, put it on a certain path, and make sure that the company is on that rightful course. You're the captain of the ship in a sense, and you'll be steering this forward to a direction that you want it to be in.

Now, you might be really good at doing that in your own life. If that's the case, then congrats, you already have a bit of a hand in your own control and being a leader. But often, most of us struggle with being the leader of our own life, to be doing what we feel is right, to be happy with the results that we get from our hard work.

Do you feel like life is just passing on by, that you're not doing what you want in life, and because of that, the aspect of living is almost too stressful for you sometimes? Do you constantly feel like you're about to explode because of this, that it is just overwhelming you and making you feel like you're out of control all the time? That might mean that you're not being the leader of your life that you so want to be, and that can play a major role in what your future might end up becoming.

For most of us, being a leader is something that we might not even contribute to our own life. We might believe that most leaders are those you see in businesses, in various other endeavors and enterprises, and you don't have to do that. Well in truth, you do need to do it in order to be successful.

Your life can go whatever way you want it to go. Being a leader of your own life is steering your life, the ship itself, into the direction that you want it to go, and from there, working to create a situation that is worthwhile, and you're doing for yourself.

Why worry about this?

You might wonder why, why you should even bother with worrying about this. Well, it's time to think about how your life is.

Are you doing what you want in life? Are you accomplishing your goals? Chances are, at least once you've said to yourself "I wish I did more." We all want to do more. We all want to succeed, but how do we accomplish this? How do we do this sort of thing?

Well, you don't do it by mulling on how to do it constantly, that's for sure. Instead, you need to become a leader. You need to take control of your life, get it on the right course, and from there, work to live the best life that you possibly can, and from there, have the results that you so desire from all of your hard work, so that you are doing what you feel is what your life desires.

There are many of us with many different problems. Unfinished goals, negativity spewing everywhere, people telling us what to believe, and what to do, all of this compounds over time. You get hit from all fronts with all of these various problems. We tend to feel all of this compound over time, and then we get sucked into the tedium of this.

With the way our society is, and with current events, it's very hard to be a leader in many cases. We feel like we're at the effect of everything that happens. We feel like we can't do anything about it, and because of that, we tend to just give up, and because of that, we don't get anywhere. That's why often, at the end of our lives, most of the time, the person on their deathbed wishes that they did more.

Now, let's not talk about the doom and gloom of this. Let's talk about why we should become leaders. We all want to accomplish what we want to in life, right? Anything from maybe finishing a huge personal project, to getting you house fixed up, to even getting a new car. You want to be the one leading your own life, and to hell with all of the other little problems that come about.

Focus Less on Others, more on yourself

We all tend to get into the problems of others. Other people are just so interesting, that we tend to really get sucked into the whole mindset of others, when we don't think about ourselves. We might think that it is bad to do this, that it's selfish, but it's actually a really good thing.

Often, we tend to sacrifice our own problems, goals, and whatever, for others. We take on the negativities of others, the goals that they have, and their problems, and it distracts us from what we want to do.

Is it selfish to focus on yourself, to work on your own personal goals, and to be happy? Course not. Sure, you should try to be empathetic to others when you need to be, but don't let the stress of others tear you down. All of us have aspirations, and we should always be working towards this.

There are many times when if you aren't doing what you want in life, it tends to overwhelm you. There are times where you just feel like nothing is worth it, simply because of the fact that you're not focusing on yourself. That's why It's important to consider your own personal issues, your own goals, your own wellness, and work on trying to better yourself. It isn't selfish to care about yourself, and you should be leading yourself down the right pathway to success, and sometimes, it's best traveled when you're not dealing with the stress and problems of other people, but instead, focusing on yourself.

Start to work on your own goals. If you have a business you want to put together, work to do it. If you have friends that are negative all the time, and you just feel bogged down, you don't have to listen to this. Start to form your life in the image that you want it to be, and it can make the world of a difference for yourself.

How do I Begin?

You might be at the point of "okay, I know that I need to be a better leader to myself, but how in the world do I start?" I say that the best way to begin is honestly, to keep on reading. We'll talk more about the pros and cons of living the life of a leader, and why you should do so, and what happens if you don't do this. I can assure you, that it will make a huge impact in your life if you do strive to become a better leader, and if you do this, you will see the difference.

But the first thing that you should do, is sit down and think about your life? Are you evading it? Is it going the way that you want it to go. You want to be totally honest with yourself, give yourself the truth and don't sugarcoat it. Instead, just say what is really going on, and how you can change this sort of course of life. It definitely is quite shocking to hear when you say, "I'm not living my life as the leader I should be" and you might feel emotional because of this. But it's not a bad thing, it's actually a good thing to realize this. Recognition is the first step, and that's what we shall focus on initially, and from there, you should then move onto the next ensuing chapters on how to become a better leader to your own life, whether it be from changing your goals, to even the company that you keep.

being a leader is a scary thing to many people, but you know what's scarier? Being a follower to your own life. Not doing what you want to in life, and instead being at the mercy of others. To be holding back your true potential because you're afraid of what society might think, or even because you're just scared of the consequences. It's time that you take better control of your life, to work in the way that you want to, shaping your life into the mold that you strive to be. For many people, this can change them drastically, from feeling like they aren't bogged by people anymore, to even feeling like they're accomplishing more with their goals because of this. Being a leader might seem like such a small thing, but for many people, this can be novel. A lot of us don't play the leader role, even in life, relying on others to do it instead of taking life by the horns and driving it in the direction we want it to go. This can be quite shocking, almost too real for many, and if you're worried about that, then you should continue reading on. We'll go over next how goals can be a huge part, and you'll also learn more about yourself and if you are leading your own life or not in the ensuing chapters.

Knowing what leading your own life is can save your life, put you on the right pathway, and in turn change you for the better.

Chapter 2: Are You Leading your own Life

Now you might wonder if you are leading your own life? You might know for sure, and we might be doing that sort of thing. Most of the time though, we're not. However, this chapter will give you the full rundown on if you are, and you should really take the time to actually think about this.

What it means to be a leader is simple. That you're your own authority, you're independent in terms of thinking, your life the way you want, and you are genuine in what you want to do with it. Now, whether it's popular, cool, or trendier, you do what you want in life, and you do what you feel is right for yourself. If you are you're leading your life the way that you are, doing what you want, whether or not people like you for it, or hate you for it, you actually have a lot more freedom than you think.

Being your own leader means that you have your inner freedom, and you maintain that, harnessing it, and you actually feel like there is a power there. You have control, and you've got your own power.

Remember, you live on a planet with almost seven billion people. Despite the fact that there are so many, everyone is different. There won't be some sort of clone coming around, but rather, the life that you have is your own, and there will never be another that's like that. Your own qualities, characteristics, what you like and don't like, and even what you strive to be, are all unique to you. If you put your mind to it, you can be whatever you want to be, and you can do what you really want in your heart if you actually do realize that you've got this power.

However, in many cases, we tend to hold ourselves back. We might not use the power that we're given, the creativity that we're bestowed, and we tend to live right on the straight line that we're given. We're afraid to take our risks that we want to, and because of that, we don't do what we want in life.

Often, it's because of a fear. A fear of being unpopular, alone, not liked or accepted, and in general, just afraid to branch out. Because of this, we tend to compromise our own uniqueness to be something that we aren't, to hold ourselves back from the true potential that we have, and because of that, we also tend to do things we don't want to do.

Have you ever done something that you regret? Or say something that you regret? Maybe you didn't take a job opportunity or go for something because you were afraid of taking a risk? That actually falls right into the category of this. This also involves not behaving in a means that is right for themselves, that is honest, and because of this, it will tend to compound as well. Later in life, usually when they're too old to do much, regret will set in. They regret not taking those risks, believing in themselves, or doing what they want to do and compromising their own personal feelings because they are afraid of what they could've been. They were afraid to take a risk.

If you have ever felt this way, then it might be the case of you're not your own leader, at least not yet. Don't be scared. It happens to a lot of us, and many of us are guilty of this. But, it's important to realize that we do have these regrets, and we don't really realize that we're doing something wrong when we betray ourselves like that, often not until it is too late.

Do you Like Yourself?

This is actually a question that might make you immediately go to the various aspects that make you feel self-conscious, but that's not what we're going for here. Look at yourself, the person that you've become, the one that you should be loving, and ask yourself, do you love yourself? Do you care about yourself, doing what you feel is right, cherishing yourself enough to be the person that you want to be, to live up to the aspirations that you have, to follow your own tune, and to treat yourself with the kindness that you should be treating yourself with?

Do you actually take the time to learn from your mistakes, realizing when you do mess up and learning from that? Do you keep on going despite how hard it might be, or how lonely you might be? If you really do, you are your own leader. But for many of us, this is a rude awakening. Lots of us don't really love ourselves enough to do what we feel is right, which is an unfortunate symptom of this.

This is a question to really ask yourself if you've been stuck on whether or not you're your own leader. You definitely should look at this, and you should do a true assessment on who you are.

Your decisions

The decisions as a leader aren't based on someone else. Sure, you can deduce a conclusion from what others have done, but at the end of the day, if you want to be a leader to yourself, you should decide on everything for yourself, and by the feelings that you possess, not what anyone else believes.

That means that you believe in what you want to believe in, deciding what is right for you, what feels right in many cases, deciding the values and the code of conduct that you should have. You also decide your morals and ethics, including what you feel is right and wrong. That might not be true for someone else, but that is something you will have to realize. Being your own leader means staying true to yourself, and following your own ethics.

Now, this also involves actually deciding what to think about things, and actually using your head. One key part of this, is critical thinking. Do you think critically? For many of us, we tend to follow what the other say, the call of others, and just blindly agree with everything. If that is the case, then you're not being a leader, for being a leader does involve actually thinking for yourself, evaluating the statements that come in, and choose what you think is right and what to believe. This also doesn't mean to think blindly, but also to look at every piece of information that is out there, and think if it's true for you. False information is you there, and if we know it's false, but still chose to believe it, then you're not being a leader. Actually, go against the values of others if you think that it is wrong, if you think everyone is just robotically following the system. Actually, decide what your life will be.

Choose what you want to do in life, and what you want to create. You should then choose the values and choices along with the thinking that will allow you to have the foundation that you want.

Now, if someone tells you to be something, or to do something, as a leader, tell them that you don't have to do anything. You don't have to choose some sort of predetermined pathway, but you're actually creating your own choices and what you want to be. You should do what you feel is right.

If there are people that are just blindly following the leader, you shouldn't do that. Be the leader of your own life. Even if this means that you're risking the aspect of being alone, not liked, not popular, rejected, or whatever it might be, it's better to do this than to just blindly follow someone, because in that case, you are being true to yourself, and true to your own desires.

What's very interesting about this as well, is that when you do what you feel is right, being the own leader that you feel that you should be, you'll start to realize that in many cases, people tend to like you more. All of those times that you didn't step out of your shell, doing what you feel is right in life, could've actually held you back, because often, it means that there is a chance that you didn't do what your heart says to do. What you should always do, is follow your own determined pathway, being the leader that you should be, and don't be afraid of what others might think. People will talk. So, what? It's not your monkey, not your circus. Deal with what you want to deal with, and to hell with the naysayers that say otherwise.

Now, another interesting thing about this, is let's say that you don't agree with a friend, and you go off to do something. Let's say that your parents want you to be something, and you want to choose that other thing. At the very beginning, there is always that risk of losing the person that you care about, whether it be the friend, or the family member, or even that support. You might walk down a lonely road. But, you can say to yourself that you're doing it, that you're being true to yourself. Plus, over time, the realization that you're doing what is right for you starts to dawn onto everyone, which means that you're doing what is right, and people will start to follow. People that aren't their own leaders yet will flock to you, because they realize that you seem to know what you're doing. Your parents who might be upset that you chose that pathway, will see that you're successful and it's because that you're authentic. You're doing what is right for yourself and you're not sugarcoating anything. Same with the friend. They might even come back to you over time.

If you're actually doing something for yourself, others will flock to you. People like to see this. For those that aren't leaders yet, they will come to you because you're demonstrating that you're brave, and that you can be yourself, determining your own fate as well. You should then, if you start to get followers, tell them to be their own leader as well. While having some followers is great, it's important to start forging others into being leaders as well. They might be scared, but just tell them that it is scary, but it's also worth it, that being your own leader is definitely worth all of the struggles that you've gone through, because at the end of the day, at the end of your life, it actually will leave you with less regrets, and more happiness of your own existence.

Now, it is easy to become a follower. It's so easy to just follow someone else, but are you really doing what you want at that point? Are you doing what makes you happy. Since it is less effort, it might seem like the easy way out, but when you're your own leader, everything isn't an effort at that point. You just know what you'll choose, knowing the answers that you have for the questions at hand, and you're doing what you want. Plus, let's think about it for a second: has anything great ever came out of just conforming to a person, not leading your own life and doing your own personal aspirations, accomplishing what makes you happy? Nothing. You're not getting anywhere just blindly following the leader. You won't be happier just conforming to the knowledge of others, and you won't be able to really grow as a person. So realize that, and take it with you.

If you ever wonder whether or not you're truly a leader of your own life, look at yourself. Are you happy? If the answer is no, then maybe start to change our life around a tiny bit, and you'll realize the difference it makes immediately.

Chapter 3: The Benefits of Leading Your Own Life

What are the benefits of finally living your own life, marching to the beat of your own drum, and doing what makes you happy without even thinking about the criticism from others? Well, let's talk about that.

For many of us, we struggle with being different, all throughout our life. It can be anything from the color of our skin, the way that we look, or even what we like and don't like. For many of us, the childhood ridicule for moot problems such as glasses, having a certain look, or even liking something, sits with us, and often, it can drive us crazy. Many times, struggling to fit in starts to become the forefront of our life, and that doesn't make you happy. For many of us, trying to fit into molds where we don't belong will stress you out, and it won't make you feel good. But what happens if you start to live your own life, accept the fact that you are different, and say to hell with the negativity that others have, living life in your own way? Well, we'll discuss this, and why it's important to be the person that you should be.

The first benefit to living your life the way that you want to, is you'll stop living in fear of what others will think. All throughout life, if we're not being our own leader, we kind of hold ourselves back in fear of being the person that we want. It's human nature to fear what others think, and whether or not you'll be judged, rejected, or even disliked and alone, and often, it prevents you from being yourself. Humans are afraid of being alone, but sometimes, being alone is better, and it will allow you to accept yourself for who you are, doing what you feel is right, and that gives you a huge sense of freedom. Often, we try our best to appease everyone, creating this huge group of friends, and often, we stifle ourselves in order to keep ourselves friends with everyone. But of course, the truth of the matter is that if you are doing that, you're not really being yourself. Instead, try to be someone that you are, not someone that you're not. It's exhausting to keep up that fake image, but being true to yourself is a courageous action, and it will be something that will allow you to be the person that you want to be, despite the urge to change you from the world. When you start to realize that your life is better being yourself instead of pleasing others, you'll be free.

It also will change the way you connect with others. Do you feel like you really truly have a strong friendship with others? Do you feel like people only like you because of fake actions, not really fulfilling the obligation of being a friend, and once you try to be yourself, they run away? Often, many people don't realize that the reason why you have these people come and go is because they aren't able to accept the real you. However, if you start to live your life, and those from your past self still stick around, you'll begin to realize that those are true friends. There are many that will only be around because of superficial matters, but if you have the right people come in and the ones that care about you stick around when you are true to yourself, the relationships that you are fulfilling are definitely truer than before. You're not living a lie, which is definitely something that you should consider.

A big part of getting others to accept you for your flaws, is to not be afraid to be yourself, and you'll realize that while you might have less friends, it actually works out better, because those that do stick around, will definitely love you for the person that you are.

A big benefit to living your own life, being the leader that you are, is that you will be a lot happier, and you will treat yourself a lot better. A big part of trying to conform is that when you do something that might not be what you like, you tend to beat yourself up. Negative self-talk is a huge part of this, and sometimes, when you're not being who you really are, the negativity from others tends to compound over time. People don't accept you for who you are, and you start to build up this fake personality, and in turn, you'll start to put yourself down for not doing what you want. Plus, many times the ones who you pull in when you're not being yourself tend to have differing opinions, and if they're overly negative, then you're going to feel that negativity. In truth, one of the best benefits of this is that you'll care a lot more about yourself, treat yourself a lot better, and stop calling yourself terrible names, such as worthless and bad because you are different.

Everyone is different. Everyone is weird, but if you accept that, you'll start to realize that it's not a bad thing. If you feel like you can't have a relationship because of who you are, then it's time to look at the personality that you're putting forward, and start to change your outlook on life by truly being what you are. Be true to yourself, accept yourself for who you are, and become the liberating person that you know you can be. It's nice when you pull yourself out of this, because it can make you feel happier than you have ever felt before.

Another significant benefit to this, and one that can really help if you just feel starved in terms of what to do next, is that you'll be able to find that passion that you have, the desire that you might have, and you'll be able to find this again. Oftentimes, when we're wallowing in the need to conform to others, we aren't really looking at ourselves, and because of that, we're not working on our own strengths, the happiness that we might have, and even using the skills that we possess to help others. For many of us, this means that we're totally selling ourselves short, not looking at what we can do, the passions at hand, and even doing what we love.

Do you feel like you're doing what you love? If the answer to that is no, then start to change yourself. Look at what you feel like your own personal strengths are. Maybe you like helping others, and you haven't really don't that in a long time? Maybe you realize that you're more cut out for social work than anything else? Start to learn a bit more about yourself, and it can make a huge difference. Once you learn about it, start to use these skills to your best of your ability. If you love to help animals, then start to volunteer at the local shelter. Maybe even start a blog about them, or even work with the shelter to put up creative ads to help these guys get adopted. Whatever it might be, do what you feel is right. If you find your passion, you'll be able to do what you love, and you'll be happy.

This especially fits if you're in a situation where you utterly hate your job. Nine times out of ten, people will complain about how bad their job is, and how they wish they could be doing something else. Well, what is that something else? Even if it is just a minor gig while you're still working our current job, actually being able to work towards your passion will make you happier, and you'll be good at it, and plus you'll love what you do.

Finally, you'll appreciate yourself. Many times, we really don't appreciate the people we've become, how far we've been able to reverse, and actually realize how different we are, appreciating that. Many times, in the past, we've been shamed for being introverted, for not talking to others, for being different, but if you actually embrace this, appreciating this for what it is, you'll be able to realize that you do enjoy this sort of thing. For those that are introverts, it will let us be creative. If we realize that we work better alone, we can get more done. Don't force yourself to do things you don't want to do. If you sit here, realizing the person that you are, the strengths and the weaknesses that you possess, you'll be able to figure yourself out for the better, and being who you truly are.

This is especially important if you start to assess your own weaknesses. We all have this. This is something that can be a hard road to come to terms with. We don't want to be weak, but if we realize that they're there, making yourself the person that you are, and you start seeing your weaknesses more as strengths than weaknesses, you'll begin to learn to appreciate yourself a lot more. You'll feel more confident, much happier, and overall having a more fulfilling life.

A final benefit to this, is that you actually can help with a whole myriad of health problems. For starters, let's take the fact that not being yourself can be exhausting and depressing. Have you ever felt like that? The fact that you just are depressed with the person that you have become. Well depression will leave your immune system open to invaders at times, and the stress of that isn't healthy either, since it will in turn also leave you wide open to any harm that might come about, including various pathogens and such. Plus, stress puts more strain on your blood pressure and your heart, and often, this can be a huge problem down the road.

But let's also look at the fact that health-wise, you probably aren't doing that well. If you're living the life of someone that you don't feel like you are, no doing what makes you happy, the compounding of this will only beget more regrets, and it will make you feel depressed, which in turn can compromise your immune system, stress you out, and you'll suffer from depression, which can, if you're not strong enough to take care of this, will lead to suicide. That is obviously a very lofty problem, and it is a rare circumstance, but being true to yourself does have that extent.

It also can affect your energy levels too. Do you just go through life exhausted and feel like you're really not doing what you want in life? If the answer to that is a resounding yes, then you need to take a minute and realize what you are saying. Your energy levels are kaput, and because of that, you aren't using enough of your energy for what you want, so you still feel tired. You're also not happy too, which will make the exhaustion worse. All of this can add up every time, and it can make you feel as if you're going mad because of how you feel. You won't be happy if you don't face the facts, become true to yourself, and are overall working towards bettering yourself.

That is why you should be your own leader. All of these benefits are there, and in general, you'll truly be happier too. I definitely have seen this in my own life, and I will say this, it is scary. It's terrifying to just up and leave the normal life that you might have put together, and you might wonder if it's even possible to accomplish this. But, would you rather do what you feel is right, or continue to hold yourself back, stifling your potential? Obviously, the answer is there, you've just got to figure it out for yourself, doing what you feel is right.

Chapter 4: What Happens if You're Not Leading Your Own Life

So how do you know you're not leading your own life? What happens when you don't? If you feel like leading your own life isn't possible, then there might be a few things that might end up happening. There might be times where you feel like you don't know where to go, where nothing seems to go the way you want it to. Perhaps you used to believe in God or a divine power, but now you don't even know for whatever reason. You might feel this way, and you might wonder if you're truly living your life. If you're wondering what might happen if you choose not to work on living your own life, if you decide to forgo all that's been said here, then you're about to find out.

Obviously, we've all been there at some point, which is why I strive to talk about being your own leader. But what are some telltale results that you're not living your own life? What happens if you continue to ignore advice, trying to follow the crowd, and in general don't decide to be the leader that you know you can be? Well, you're about to find out just what will happen as a result of these actions.

The first thing that will happen is that you will begin to notice that you are floundering, really just unable to control your life. You feel like you're just kind of living the life you've made for yourself. You don't feel like you're not really stimulated anymore, and it makes you feel critical and crabby. You might notice that you're frustrated all the time, and if you don't choose to become the leader that you want to be, you'll notice that nothing seems enjoyable, and you'll feel like you're just kind of living life. You want the change, but you don't know where to begin. Simply put, you're like a fish on dry land, literally floundering in hopes that you can get back to the water to live. If you feel like you're stagnant like this, this is a result of no taking control of your own life.

If you do not try to become the leader of your own life that you want to be, you're going to feel this stagnation, and for many, it's literal hell on earth. Keeping yourself occupied and able to figure out what to do with yourself is actually a very important part. Living your own life will allow you to take an honest look at every single part of yourself, working to let go of anything that is a problem for you, and from there, you'll become the leader that you want to be. Stagnation is a sign that you have to change, and this is often a result of the utmost refusal to lead.

You notice this as well, that those aggravations that have been sitting there for a long time will continue to aggravate you if you don't take leadership and work on leading your own life. Do you ever notice at times that if you're trying to sell something, it won't sell, or you're arguing with others constantly? You might feel like you're always failing, that you don't have enough money, or you're just not happy? If all of these things seem to be happening, they're not just little challenges and headaches that will cause you problems, it's also a sign that mentally something is off, and you need to be taking an honest look at yourself. You should definitely look down at yourself and see what is going on, what you're refusing to be true to yourself over. Maybe it's the fact that you need a career change, because you just feel so uninspired from the work that you're currently doing, and because of that, you'll start to notice that you feel a new drive or something. Maybe you feel like the spice in your marriage is gone for a reason, and you talk it out with your partner, creating moments of peace. You'll start to notice that various actions then keep happening. Our bank balance will be higher, you've got savings, and you'll generally feel in harmony with yourself. If you're not leading a life that you want to, and instead are just floating on by in life because of all that is happening, then it's a sign that you should definitely start to look at becoming your own leader. It can change you for the better, and in turn, it can make you a much more stimulating person that you might believe you can be. You will also notice that from this, your own strength and tenacity will also increase as well, and you'll feel more resourceful with all that you're given in life as well.

Punishment is also a sign of what can happen if you're not being the leader you want to be. Do you feel like you're getting punished all the time by various life obstacles, whether they be that you've suffered from a track record with bad exes, bad illnesses, and the like? If that is the case, this can often be a sign of not taking leadership of your own life. It isn't a punishment, even though it often tends to feel like that, but it's actually a sign that you should be looking to make sure that you're doing the right thing.

Life can be hard, and often, when we're robbed of various happiness that was there before, it can often become quite hard to not just follow the crowd of "life sucks and then you die." There is so much more to it, and while you might feel like everything is a sort of punishment for yourself, it often can be a big thing to realize that it might just be a sign that you're not taking control of your life.

For example, maybe you had an ex leave you. You might realize that it is because, down the road when you take a look at yourself, that the person wasn't right for you. That you would've followed the crowd of bad relationships if you kept with this. If you feel like life is just punishing you, this can often be a sign that you're not looking at yourself and seeing the truth, not seeing what is really happening.

Plus, occasionally those punishments come forward and rear their ugly heads. If you just bested a really bad job, got out of there and started to live your own life, it can be chaotic. But, that chaos is a sign of change, a sign of new problems going away and order being thrown in. This can be seen when taking a place of leadership in your life too, and while often it can be a sign that you need to put some order into your life, to take back what's rightfully yours, you should also look into the fact that it might also come about because of the difference that you're making in your life, the difference that you're doing for yourself and for others, and exactly what it means for you as well. Do make sure that failure is seen as something, and don't just think that it's all happening because of a divine power or something.

If you don't do what you want in life, it can also affect the rest of your relationships as well. You'll pull in people that like the façade of yourself instead of your true form. They don't really care about you, they just care about the fake image that you've put forward. You'll be living the life of a lie, and this can happen as well with partners too. All too often, you see people who aren't really at the helm of their own personal control getting into relationships, only to leave the person after once they realize what they've done. If you've ever been with someone, and when you leave them you look back at the relationship and wonder what the hell you were thinking, chances are, that is a sign that the person was fitting for that façade of yourself, and not for the real you. It's true with friendships as well. You'll pull in people based on the type of person that you are.

If you're really not leading your own life, you'll get people of the same caliber. If you're the type that isn't doing the job that they love, but you've got work friends, then that might be a sign that these word friends are only your friends because of the job, or they only like you because of one thing. This is definitely something that will happen if you don't take control, you'll pull in the wrong people.

This is often how abuse cases start too. You'll be the person who is timid, fearful, and in general doesn't stand up for themselves. They get together with someone who is really rotten and not right for them, they think it's perfect, and then later on, they realize what the hell they've done, and they regret it all. This is how regret if formed, by not being true to yourself and hurting yourself in many different ways. By realizing this, you'll be able to control the company that you keep, those that you hang out with, and you'll also in turn begin to realize that you've been around the wrong crowd because you haven't taken leadership.

Another key part that demonstrates what will happen if you don't assume leadership, is confidence. Confidence is something that everyone wants to have. That confidence in yourself is a form of security, and it's something that you will enjoy. By being confident, you'll be able to take control of all that you have going for yourself, and you'll be able to use this confidence in future endeavors and the like. If you don't take control of yourself, you might realize that you've got some confidence, but it isn't the true potential that you so desire. Instead, it's a false hope that everything is fine, a false little mask that you'll put on because of this, and your confidence won't really be at the highest potential you can be at.

If you're not leading your own life, you'll be giving into others, not being true to yourself, and in turn destroying whatever confidence that you have. Confidence allows you to be sure of yourself, to take those chances, and to do what you feel is right, something that as a leader, you should always have.

If you're ever worried about the state of your confidence, actually take an honest look in the mirror at yourself and do what you feel is right for yourself. By being true to your own desires, your own goals, and your own behavior, you'll feel better than you ever have before, and you'll be much better off as well.

Confidence ties into everything; your job security, how happy you are, and it can even be a great way to ward off depression and other such problems that you might suffer from. If you've ever been worried about if you're not leading your own life, take a look at your confidence. When you don't lead your own life, and instead are at the mercy of others, it's a telltale sign, since you'll notice that you'll have less confidence, less happiness, and in turn, you'll feel a whole lot more at the mercy of the life that you have, instead of being in utter control of yourself, and the life you're been given.

Leading your own life isn't easy. I never said that it was. It's full of risks, and it can be scary to do. But when you don't live your own life, it can ultimately end up being worse for you, and if you're wondering what might happen if you choose to do otherwise, you can read here what exactly will be affected by the decision to not be in full control of your life.

Chapter 5: Checking Your ego at the Door

The first thing that you will have to learn to be the leader that you want to be, is to get rid of that darn ego. Egos are something that we all have, and while it is good to be confident being egotistical is something totally different, and something that you need to realize isn't all that it is cracked up to be. When you're egotistical, or your ego isn't controlled, that is where problems happen, and this chapter will talk about how to check the ego at the door, and the best means to do so.

Why You Gotta Chill your Ego

Now, let's talk about what the ego is, and really why you gotta control it. To begin, everyone has an ego. This is essentially you, what you're thinking, feeling, and willing, and distinguishing it from other paths of thought. This is really the part that mediates between yourself and the physical environment. However, ego also means self-importance, which you should have, but it does eventually evolve into something called conceit, which does change the way others view you. While having an ego is a great thing, since it does involve the way you look at yourself, having too much of an ego is actually dangerous, and it will stifle your learning.

Are you someone that prances around like you're the king or queen of the world? Or do you feel like you're always shirking at everything. If you do feel either of these things, it's important to take a look at your ego. Everyone has one, and it is important to understand that egos are a part of you, but you must have control over it. If you're someone that prances around like you own the place, think that you're the only person here, you often get seen as conceited, or even careless. Our ego is a part of you, but it should be controlled.

On the same front, you need to realize that our self-image doesn't have to be garbage. You can be happy with yourself. Even those with introverted tendencies do have an ego, and they do need to realize that it isn't a terrible thing, but rather a way of life, and it is important that you do help build yourself to the person you want to be, and to not just be the ego that you put forward.

Your ego is a part of you. It is very important to have some ego to yourself. Otherwise, you won't ever feel good about yourself. Have you ever seen those people that always doubt themselves, that think that it's impossible to do something? That is an ego problem within itself as well. You shouldn't try to contain this, nor should you try to force it, but you should work to manage this and understand it. Your ego is a big part of you, and it is almost like a universal concept that you need to learn. Remember, everyone is unique with a personality there, and the ego should be embraced. Regardless of if you feel like you need to check your ego, or if you need to work on our ego, you should work to see the beautiful quality that is there.

Now, the ego is something that you should keep as a part of you. Don't let it be separated, but instead, work together and tame this. How do you do that though? It can be quite hard, and you should definitely realize that your ego is a great thing, but it is also something worth honing. Your ego will allow you to improve your life, but having too much of it does paint you in a super negative light, so it should be avoided.

As a leader, your ego can be your greatest weapon, or it can be your demise. It's important to have control over this, and you need to in order to be successful.

Taming the Ego

Now, what happens if you don't tame it? If you don't take the time to realize that you screwed up on something, that you're not perfect, that you aren't the center of the universe, this actually can cause you to be so full of yourself that you succumb to it. Now, leaders need to be told no, they need to fail, and they need to realize their mistakes.

For many leaders, if they're never told this, this actually causes a dangerous mindset, where they think that they're better than everyone else. If a leader isn't tamed in terms of ego, and they don't listen to others and be open, they can definitely start to fall down.

You've probably seen it. You've seen those that have powerful egos, and they think that they're the center of the universe. They don't care about others, nor do they have compassion for the common man. If you lose this, and if you don't really look at the way others act, this can cause you to be so full of yourself that you don't really work towards a better life. You won't learn if you do this.

You've probably seen businesses that have failed because their leader only cared about themselves, that they're egotistical, that they refuse to learn. This is why people will quit jobs, why they'll just up and leave companies, and it's why some places are experiencing the downfall of a business. Realize this, and do something about it, for it can make a huge difference.

You need to listen to others, to be open, and to find wisdom in other places. We'll talk more about how you can tame your own ego in the next section, but it is important that you learn this, for it can help save your life.

How to Become a Better Leader by Controlling your Ego

So how do you do this? How do you control that pesky ego of yours so that you're not being seen as the uncaring person that you might worry people view you as? Well, it's actually relatively simple.

For starters, you need to start by not taking everything personally. Not everything is about you, and taking offense to everything is going to ruin you. If you continuously do that, you're actually in agreement with whatever is bothering you, which then leads you down this path where you feel like you need constant validation in order to keep your ego going. Some people won't like you. Simple as that. Some people might not have the best opinion of you, and that's okay. As a leader, you can't make everyone happy. There is always that one person out there that doesn't like you, but you should be working on liking yourself. This is important for those that have too big of an ego and too small. If your ego is small and you're offended by everything, guess what, your self-image is going to really stink. Don't do this to yourself, and you should instead just let others have their opinions. Don't try to change everyone.

Now, sometimes, you gotta watch what you say, and as a leader, you should do this. You should think about the words that you say, not only for yourself, but for others as well. Having a mouth that is in control, and one that will bring others up instead of one that word vomits everywhere makes a huge difference. If you do take the time to think about this, you'll be able to dictate your thoughts in a much simpler manner, and in return get the same back. You'll be able to have better dictations with others, and a much better life.

Now, don't get into the labels either. That's part of the reason why you haven't been a leader your entire life. It's because you've been so focused on what others think about you, and you haven't really been in touch with who you are. Instead, get past the identifications that are there, the labels that are forced onto you. If you've labeled yourself as something, and you feel like it doesn't fit you, then don't buy into that. Simple as that. You're not just one type of person, you're different than that. You're a person that has power, and you'll be able to take control if you start to learn to realize that you're not the labels society puts on you. The second that you stop trying to be something that society forces you to be, then you'll start to become happier.

Now, learn to control what you say. This also involves listening to others. The biggest thing that we can do in many cases is to start to control our mouths and such. It is quite hard for some of us to just shut up and listen. I know this, and I've been there. However, having control over your mouth can help with various outbursts that you have in life. You might start to notice how easy it is to have total control over this. You should start to learn how to become better with this, exercise control over it, and realize just how easy it is to hold yourself back. When someone talks, learn to listen. If you don't like what someone wears, what they say or do, or whatever, then learn to listen to them. If you don't really know what to think, sometimes keeping your mouth shut says a lot about it, and it can help with other discourses too.

Then, start to learn to be comfortable with yourself. Remember, there is nobody like you. Learn to enjoy being the person that you are. As someone that might have an inflated ego, sometimes actually sitting back, realizing that you're someone that you haven't been acting as, and actually learning to be the person that you want to be, can help quell this. For those that tend to not have a strong ego, self-image is key here. You need to stop comparing yourself to others. As a leader, always comparing will mean that you never get a chance to be yourself and spread your wings. While many times we do try to do this, it's a trick of the ego thinking that you're better or that you're worse than someone else. Stop doing that, and instead fall in love with yourself.

Your ego can be a great thing, but it can also be dangerous if left unchecked. Start to take care of this situation by working to ensure that you have control over your ego so that you're not interfering with this problem. What you need to do instead, is to start working on bettering yourself, and don't fall for the trap of your ego.

Chapter 6: Committing to Goals

Goals are a big part of being your own leader. By having goals, you'll be able to be a better person, and you'll be able to keep your life on the best track possible. This chapter will be all about goals, how to set them and how to commit to them, in order to become the leader of your own life that you strive to be.

Being specific

Now when you are looking at your goals, you should be specific, but also be long-term. You should set your goals for daily affairs, and make sure that you also look at the monthly and long-term goals. The long-term might be years down the road, but they are tied to your dreams. You shouldn't be afraid to go big, since nothing is impossible. Remember if you can believe, you can achieve. You should try to go for realistic goals that you feel like you can work towards each and every single day.

With each of these goals, don't try to make them super complicated. You can have ambitious and realistic goals, but also ones that are very simple as well. Sometimes, the simplest ones are the best goals.

For many of us, committing to goals is hard work, especially since we might not have the mentality to commit to something huge. However, by actually working towards this, actually having a goal that you want to keep at, and really committing to it will help you do it. That's why you want it to be simple, since it'll allow you to be focused and allow you to streamline the goal as well.

For many people, they sometimes feel like they want the world. Which is totally doable, but they often don't have the patience to build it up, nor do they make the goal simple enough to follow. Goals can be a lot, since they often involve changing an aspect of your life or behavior, so it's best to ensure that the goal that you maintain is one that is possible, and one that will allow you to have the best life that you can have. So be specific, but also don't try to make them super complicated.

For example, if you have a goal such as "I want to make money selling my pictures," then make that the goal. You should have that as the goal, which is simple, but then plan out how you can do this. This isn't a hard goal, it's actually pretty simple and not made to be overcomplicated. But of course, you want to have the details mapped out so that you can improve on this goal. Essentially, you want the goal to be fulfilling and engaging, specific, but also not super detailed and tedious that it isn't fun.

You should approach all of these goals like how a craftsman does, working to make a stronger, smarter, and better craft on a daily basis, working to ensure that you have the goal at hand one day at a time.

Out with the Negative, in with the Positive

One big problem with those that set goals is they want to be negative. For example, if you want to lose weight, don't say "I want to stop being fat" because that'll just perpetuate the idea and the negativities idea that you are fat. If you say, "I want to look the best I can be, so I'm going to eat right" you'll start to hear that little voice in your head constantly tell you that you're terrible, fat, and that the only way to get better is to starve yourself. Having the goal in a negative manner will only perpetuate the negative behavior. Instead, write down the behaviors and the values that you really want to focus on, and make sure that they are manifested within the ideas that you have. For example, if you have a weight loss goal, say to yourself "I'm going to eat at least one salad a day" or "I'm going to exercise for at least thirty minutes each day" whether that be a walk, run, or whatever it might be. With a goal, don't try to overload yourself with a bunch, but instead, keep it to a few so that you can focus on them.

Being positive about the goals will allow you to focus on them a lot better, and having less on your plate will allow you to set the bar to the level you so desire. Remember, simple actions get you closer to your goals. Smaller, positive waypoints that you can hit each and every day will make it much easier for you to hold yourself at the pillar of responsibility and also monitor the progress that you so have.

By doing this, formulating your actions, and being positive, you'll start to realize that you're achieving your goals. In a world that's always focusing on the negative, it can be quite hard to be positive, since that is a big problem for many people. But, if you do set your goals in a realistic manner, in a positive manner, and in a way that you'll commit, you'll feel better, and you'll feel more on track as well.

Interested or Committed

For many people, they often aren't really committed to their goals, and instead, they are interested in them. While interest is a great thing to have, the way to get committed and to achieve your goals is to simply, be committed. You should start to look at this sort of thing.

If you ever wonder whether or not you're interested or committed, first, look at yourself. Do you procrastinate on your goal, simply read stuff but never apply it, make excuses, and in general say, "that's nice" but never do anything about it?

Then you're interested. You want to do something about it, but you haven't hit the point where you've done anything about it. If you're wanting to acquire the skills to make this possible, focus on what you need to do, actually apply what you've learned to your life, and in general always have the view on this, then you are committed. Now, most of us are usually in the former category, which isn't bad per se at the onset, but if you want to get any real work done, you've got to be committed.

Now, let's say that you have the goals are laid out, everything is all neat and orderly, but you feel as if you're not able to really get involved with it. What do you do then? It's time to work on becoming committed instead of interested, and here is how you can accomplish it.

Sit down, and write down everything that is holding you back from doing this, whether it be money, peers, and the like. Actually, sit there and really write down what is making you feel like you can't reach our full potential. Now, once you have it done, tear up those things holding it back. Think about how you can commit to this. You should realize that if you really want this, you'll do something about this. You'll make it happen. If you want to explore the world, get that dream job, or have that dream house, make sure that you have a powerful enough motivator for your work. You should try to just work towards it, each and every day.

Focus on What is important

With a goal, you should focus on what is important, and what will get you to this. If you are focusing on the mundane activities that won't help you, or maybe you're not focusing on how to really implement your goal, then guess hat, you're not going anywhere.

Having a goal doesn't mean that you're going to have to slave away at something and do double the work that you did before. Instead, it's starting to put in a few little parts of it, but also not getting yourself so overloaded that you can't get anywhere. For many of us, we have lives that are full of responsibilities. But, we also have these goals. Sometimes, we think that we have to take on the huge parts of this goal immediately, but in truth, it actually isn't that. What you want to do instead, is actually focus on the very important parts, and only do a little bit of this each day.

That's right, you don't have to dedicate hours of your free time to this goal, but instead, maybe about thirty or so minutes. If you want to do more, then by all means do more, but if you really want to create the goal in your life, you shouldn't try to overload yourself, and work to create the invaluable content for the goal, simple as that. You should work to only do a little bit each day towards the goal, setting a chunk of time to do that, but then, once that time is up, go about your daily affairs. You don't have to push yourself that hard, nor do you really need to slave away at it. Goals should be fun, and you should keep them fun and simple.

Be responsible

Responsibility is probably the main reason why some people don't get started and why they don't really follow through with this. However, you need to be responsible for this, to hold yourself accountable for this whole thing, and you should definitely try to ensure that you have that in mind. By being responsible for this, you'll be constantly reminded of this, and from there, you'll be able to work at it all the time, and you'll have a reason to go forward.

A common mistake that everyone seems to have is the fact that they don't actually take responsibility for it. They think that it'll magically fall into their hands without any hard work. News flash: it does take hard work, dedication, and goals. You have to make sure that you hold yourself responsible for what you do, and actually work towards it.

There are a few things that you can do to actually get this into place, to take responsibility for being a leader. First, is to have a goals system to help keep track of what you're doing. On Sunday, write down your goals for the week, and before bed each night, write down a couple of tasks that will help you get to these goals. You can then get them done the next day, and go to bed without feeling guilt. Plus, it'll make you happier, since you'll be closer to your goals.

Next, talk to others. Tell your family and close friends what you're doing. If the goal is a confidential one, keep it to a few family members that you can trust. You should tell them about it, and you should keep reminding them of that. One thing to know is that you might get reactions that aren't totally supportive. However, don't take that as a sign to give up, but instead, take that as a sign that you need to stay committed. Let their disdain for it keep you motivated and committed. Even if it's to prove that you're doing the right thing, it can make a world of a difference.

Finally, find people that are similar in thought to you. These like-minded people will root for you, and the fact that they care about your success can make a world of a difference. You'll get the confidence and the motivation needed, and from there, you'll take your business to the next level, which is something that we all should strive to do.

All of these factors will allow you to set your goals, achieve them and really commit to them. By doing this, you'll be able to ensure that you're getting the best results possible, and you'll be able to do a whole lot for yourself if you work towards this. Setting goals is the first step to success, and the first step towards being the leader you want to be. You can do this, and by sticking to the information here, you will be successful.

Chapter 7: Ways to Become a Better Personal Leader

There are a few ways to help become a better personal leader in your own life. When it comes to leading, sometimes it's more than just goals. There are a few things that you can do in order to help make this better, and this chapter will help you become better at this subject, to the point where you're happy with the results at hand.

Becoming a Better Example

One of the biggest things that can help you become a better personal leader, is to have the idea that you should lead your life by better examples. Remember, every single day you are setting an example to others, whether you realize it or not, whether it be positive or negative. You should try to show to others that you are a good example.

This is important to being your own leader, because if you're not following your own code, doing what you feel is right, and being your own leader, you won't be taken seriously in some cases by your peers. If you set a good example, others will follow, since they see you as a leader. You should always try to be the best example that you can be, even if it isn't easy for you to do. It won't be, but it's better than just following the crowd and not being the best person that you can be.

Being Humble

Being humble is probably one of the hardest things for us. We all want to be seen in the spotlight, and you should definitely make sure that you take the credit and validation when it is due. But, sometimes you have to be humble. Bring others up, and if you do something, and others follow it, make sure that the credit is given where it's due. Sometimes, being your own leader doesn't always mean trying to be in the spotlight all the time, it's showing to others that you're a better person, that you're happier by helping others, and you should try to showcase that while you are doing your own thing, you should definitely give credit to people if they do help you.

Remember, on the journey to being a better leader, you will have your own core beliefs and such. But, if you do get help from another person, do try to ensure that you do give them the validation and the recognition for helping them. By doing this, you'll be setting a better example, and showing that you are a better personal leader to yourself.

Don't be Scared

Fear is probably one of the biggest hurdles of being a leader. We all get to that point in life when we feel like running away. When we're not being leaders, we tend to stay in our lane, our bubble, and because of that, we never try to work to improve ourselves. Be bold and courageous. Sometimes, we will fall down, we will mess up, and sometimes, we might have trouble getting back up. But, being willing to learn from your mistakes, getting up, and going at it again will allow you to learn from it. Don't be afraid to take that chance sometimes. You might never know what you might get you of it.

Sometimes, when you lead in life, and when you want to be the best personal leader that you can be, you need to do things that are scary, that make you feel fear, and things that might be a risk. But, think about all of that courage that you're about to bring unto yourself because of it. Being a better leader does involve this, and it's a surefire way to make sure that you're doing what you feel is right, and doing what makes you happy as well.

Embracing Change

Change is something that comes with being a leader. Simply put, when you lead, you're bringing about change, whether it be to your life, or to the lives of others, and frankly, it's quite scary. You might be afraid of implementing that new idea, or doing something out of the boundaries that you're comfortable with. Trust me, I've been there. Trying something new to cater to your own personal goals isn't the easiest thing out there, but it definitely can help you get better with time.

If a new opportunity comes forward that fits your goals, if you want to take on a new business venture that is worth the risk, if you're willing to work on something new with other people that will certainly work, then go ahead, work on that, and see if that will change your life. Remember, it might seem impossible now, it might seem hard, but at the end of the day, if you take life by the horns, working to make sure that you have the best life possible, you'll start to realize that these new ideas and opportunities aren't just something pretty that you can talk about, but also something that will help you become a better person at the end of the day. Do what you feel is right, and if that means taking a risk, working on some new opportunity, or the like, then by all means, do that, since it is right for you.

Do what's right for you, even if others don't like it

Now, sometimes you might run into that situation in life where others are doing something that they believe is right, but you don't really feel like that works for you. This is often a common moral dilemma, and often, it can be quite cumbersome to deal with. If you're worried about doing the right thing, really ask yourself if that aligns with the goals that you have in mind, and if that is something that is part of your integrity. Now, when it comes to your own personal ethics and such, there isn't a compromise there. You should always do and say what you believe is part of our alignment, and part of your life. By doing this, you'll be able to have a much better idea of what you're going for. It's important that you keep your integrity in, since that is often the first thing that will go out when trying to be a leader.

It's hard to fight with your own integrity at hand, because often it can be different from the societal norm. But, it doesn't have to be rough, and you don't have to be mean about it, just stand your ground. Remember, we all aren't perfect, and sometimes you might be wrong about something, but keeping your integrity at the helm of yourself, and not losing sight of it, can be some of the best things that you can do. If you choose what's right for you over what is conventional and right for others, you'll realize that you feel a lot better, and you'll get a lot of benefits from it as well. So, do what you feel is best for you, what you feel is right, and from there, you'll begin to realize that it is a lot better for you as well.

Respect yourself

One of the key things that you need to learn, is to respect yourself. Sometimes, it's hard to do this, because we often put ourselves at the back of our minds even when we don't really mean it. But, sometimes generating respect can be a huge part of this, and it can make a huge difference in your life as well.

If you're doing something that isn't beneficial to your own survival, or your body, then knock it off. Don't keep subjecting yourself to the torture that you're putting your body through, and don't keep pushing your body into this type of lifestyle.

What you got to do instead, is start working towards a better respect for yourself, a better life for yourself, and work to create a better lifestyle for yourself too. If you do this, and if you do take the time to really think about what you're doing to yourself, you can actively change your life.

Sometimes, this can be as simple as not actively drinking all the time, or even just making sure that you take care of your body. If your goal is to lose weight and be a better leader in that aspect of your life, respect yourself and get yourself some healthier alternatives. If you work towards benefitting your own health and your own life, you'll be a lot happier as well, and you'll realize as well that things are a lot easier if you take the time to really work on making yourself the best person that you can be.

So, respect yourself. Cater to your own personal goals and wellness, and from there, make sure that you're doing the right thing for yourself, and for others too, since this can be a huge part of it. Be the change that you want to see in life, the change that you feel is right, and from there, you'll be a lot happier at the end of the day, since you are respecting the wishes of yourself.

Be around Better People

Better people might seem like something obvious, but it actually makes a big difference on being a better leader to yourself and to others. For many of us, we tend to surround ourselves with people that are negative if we are negative. If we're positive, then we will bring in the positive people. This is pretty obvious, but it's part of the reason why so many who want to lead their own life struggle.

If you want to have a better life, sometimes the first place to look is the company that you keep. Look at the people that you're around. Are they negative? Are they smart and more experienced? If you have people that are smarter or more experienced than you, then you'll tend to grow a lot more. If you're around people that bleed out positivity, then you'll be much more positive as a result of this. This is something that you'll begin to realize is a huge part of it. Sometimes, the best way to have growth and development is to look at the people that you surround yourself with, and start to look into maybe keeping different company if you begin to realize that they aren't the good people that you expect them to be. You'd be surprised how, as a leader, you're changing the way your life is by the people that you surround yourself with, and sometimes, that's really the simplest thing, and it can make a huge difference in your life as well.

By being around positive people, you'll also be happier too. It's also encouraged to be around the people that challenge you, that help you go towards your goals, that will allow you to feel better about yourself as well. By being able to really ensure that you have the best life that you can possibly have, then you'll be able to create and fester a better existence for yourself, and you'll become the leader that you want to be.

Be the leader that you want to be. Keep these in mind. Work on bettering yourself, and if you feel like your experience is stifled for whatever reason, start to look at the company that you keep, the people that you surround yourself with. Sometimes, if you don't realize that the people you're around are toxic, then it can create a major difference in the life that you have. By being able to bring yourself to a better existence through the use of these techniques, you'll become a better leader to yourself. A leader will lead others, and when you're a better leader to yourself, you'll bring about a better leader to others as well.

You'll challenge the status quo of society, making yourself a better person, and from there, you'll feel much better about yourself, and how others regard you as well. Do that, and you'll surely win.

Chapter 8: Why you should Question Everything

One thing that a leader should always do is question everything. Whether it be something as small as a company record, or even something as huge as a belief, you should always try to question everything, and it can make a world of a difference in the state of our leadership. Why should we even bother to do this though? What will we get from this? Well, you're about to find you, since this chapter will go into further detail on what it means to question everything, and why you should do so when you're trying to be a better leader.

A world of Deceit

Have you ever listened to someone online, or maybe even in person, spout a whole bunch of false information, and the people immediately fall for it hook, line, and sinker? That is a common problem, and in our society, with the way the media is, and how conflicting papers seem to completely change the story around, it can make the idea of fabrication much more obvious. Fabrication is the name of the game in many cases, with the intent of deceit, err and even trying to make people dumber. That's right, this information is sometimes used to make people dumber than they really are, and often, people don't realize that this is the game that they're trying to play.

Plus, in our world today, we almost feel smothered by the need to just stay on the same path, not really trying to question anything, and that actually is why people don't progress. You might wonder why sometimes science doesn't move forward, and why people don't take a leadership position? Well, it's because they don't question it.

But in order to grow as a person, develop better habits, actually hone your talents, and learn more about life, you need to take in more information, question the validity of it, and in general learn to question everything. You can actually learn more, become a smarter person, and even grow as a human if you do manage to develop any sorts of questioning means. You should definitely learn to question life, and as a leader, it is essential.

To be a leader, it means that you need to follow your own path, being your own leader and benefitting from what you know. That means, not taking people's opinions and facts at face value, but instead really cultivating your own learning by actually asking if that is the case. You might be afraid of doing this, and that is a common problem with this, but it actually can stifle you if you're not careful.

Why we don't question

You might wonder why we don't question everything, and why this is a common problem. Sometimes, it's because we fear that we are indeed intruding on someone, or that it might cause confusion, and the ridicule that might be a part of this. Often, if we're afraid to be challenged, we become arrogant in our own beliefs, and sometimes, we fear that we might be too arrogant, which is what stifles many of us.

In the past, actually questioning anything was a key part of science, and it is part of the reason why people stifled their understanding of life. They were afraid to actually question it all, since it could mean that they might have to repress in order to keep the peace, and to keep the power as well.

Questioning society was often met with death in many cases, such as in the case of the olden times where if you even dabbled in science and questioned the universe, you actually were met with imprisonment or death. Galileo was a prime example of this, since he was insistent upon the sun being at the center of the universe, and people were against that idea. However, he had courage to fight this sort of thing. It is scary, and while we do live in an age where it's easier to question stuff, there is still the worry that there might be people ready to denounce, threaten you, or even get mad because you're questioning the authenticity of this. You have to understand that utter truth is often hard to fight with logic and scrutiny in many cases, but questioning stuff will allow you to determine whether something is right or wrong, and it will allow you to shape your beliefs.

As a leader of your own life, you might get some information about what you're doing that is questionable. People will come forward and tell you how to live your life, that your goal should be to go to college, get a desk job, and have a kid or two after you get married. But that doesn't have to be the case. That doesn't have to be the sole reason for your existence, and it never has to be. What you need to do, is learn to question stuff, even when there is the chance that things could go south.

How Questioning Creates Confidence

Questioning is something that can be quite scary, and it can be something that can definitely be quite hard on many people. Sometimes, questioning stuff takes a lot of courage, since often, it means that you might end up being wrong, and you need to get over the fear of being wrong to learn more. You should also start to become more modest about the criticisms. You shouldn't hold your thoughts on the highest pedestal, but you should also be willing to take a stand when you need to and question. Sometimes, by questioning, you have a better chance at creating some useful ideas that will help to make mankind the best that it can be.

If you do learn something, or if you question something, you should always be humble, since often this can be quite hard for others to accept. The idea of being narrow-minded is a common problem with many conventional individuals, and sometimes, people will actually defend these conventional ideas to the very end. You might be shocked at how the human nature changes as well, since often this can be quite hard for others to accept. You should, as a person, learn to question authority when you feel it is right, question why you do stuff, and in general, be a better learner by taking the time to understand the ideas of others a bit more. Questioning authority, life, and in general, can help you become a much better person, and it will allow you to have a better idea of what it is that you need to do.

Remember, we don't know everything. Nobody does. It's important to realize that you are living in a world where not everyone knows everything about anything, and it is important to understand that there is always that chance that you're wrong, or they're wrong. When working to better yourself, don't be afraid to admit simply, that you're wrong. It is a big part of it.

We do live in a life where we try to avoid various wars and such, where we have a government that is always trying to push forward paths for us, that it's hard to get out of the status quo that we've been bestowed, but remember, you don't know everything. You have a right to question everything that you come across. You should try to understand the questions that are given to you, and actually work to ask important questions, since it'll be how we make a change for ourselves and for others.

We should work to become better people that are passionate. But remember, questioning stuff is always important to help you understand. Remember, if you're working towards a goal, and there is something that you need to understand better, question it. Don't be afraid to find out more information, challenge an authority, and in general learn to question everything that is happening to you. You'd be surprised at how much you know or even don't know because of this.

There is a lot out there that we don't understand, a world out there that we don't get. There are many things that we seem to think we know, but we really don't, and this can be grounds for questioning. But, if you worry about being too arrogant, actually step back, sit there, work on questioning yourself and authority, and do what you feel is right. Do what you believe is best, and do what you feel is utterly possible for yourself. You'd be surprised at how different your life will be if you start to work on questioning everything.

How to Question as a Leader

There are a few ways that you can learn to question when it comes to being a leader, and that's what we'll discuss here. You might not know how to even begin with this sort of thing, or even where to get started, but let's start by giving you a few ways to truly question, in order to understand life a lot better.

First, if you start to notice that there is something amiss about maybe some fact that you find on the internet, start to research it a bit better. If someone is over there spouting facts about something that are questionable, start to look for the answer on a search engine, and from there, you can then start to formulate your own opinion. Don't be afraid to tell others about this as well. However, remember that they might not be on the same side as you, and they could get upset, so be ready to be reproached if the other person hears about it.

Next, learn to read a bit more on every single subject. Whenever you do research something, do try to break it down a bit more as you go along. Don't be afraid to sit there and try to work on it yourself. You'd be surprised at how different everything is if you sit down and actually dissect this whole thing. You can do so by ensuring that you're able to really look deeply into the situation, look at the reasons behind why a person might think this way, and definitely do take all of these factors into consideration when you do decide to formulate an opinion.

Also, when you do this, don't be afraid to speak up. If you see someone obviously spouting something wrong, don't be afraid to correct them. They might be mad that you're doing this, but if you think about it, if you talk to them about it now, it'll be easier on you as well. You'll feel better about it, about yourself, and really just about anything if you do take the time and realistically look at the situation from your own viewpoint.

Finally, be ready to admit that you were wrong if you have had this stable opinion that ends up being wrong. Being wrong isn't the worst thing in the world, that's for sure. It can sometimes be a bit nerving, since it does mean that you weren't correct about something, but it's better to be wrong and learn more, than to always have an ego and think that you're right about everything. That can be quite a hard pill to swallow, but often, it means that you've learned more about yourself, and you're more than willing to become a better person.

Start to take the time to learn to question things. Questioning isn't this terrible thing that you shouldn't do, but rather it's something that you should try to do all the time. Encourage yourself to learn more about others, to learn more about your life, and to be happy, for it can change the way you lead yourself. Remember, at the end of the day you don't know everything. That is the truth of it, and sometimes, stepping back and humbling yourself, learning about it and realizing that you might've been wrong about something, can be hard, but at the end of the day, it can make a world of a difference in your life, and the lives of others as well.

Chapter 9: How to Appreciate the Good as a Leader

When it comes to being a better leader, sometimes it does involve appreciating the good in life, and not focusing as much on the bad. Appreciating what you have in life is a bit hard for some, but for others, it can make a world of a difference. This chapter will dive further into this, including what it means for you to do this, and why you need to learn to appreciate what you have in life, in order to become the happiest person that you can be.

A world Full of Negativity

Sometimes, we get swamped into the negativity of the world. In all honesty, it is hard out there. With the way our current social and political climates are, it's hard to not be negative, and often, negativity is a key element of many people.

Have you ever been around someone that is negative, seeping into your own life, making you feel like everything is negative? That is a problem with many these days. We get pulled into the urge to follow, and because of that, we're always focusing on the negative influences of the world instead of the positivity.

When it comes to our thoughts, it can take literally one negative thought to throw us off. Have you ever experience that? Where you're doing great and then one day, you end up with some super negative thought that ruins your entire day? That is the problem. We let our negative thoughts take over, and we often don't appreciate the good in life.

We take this for granted. We take everything in our life for granted in some way, shape or form. For example, have you ever thought about every time you say "thanks" to someone? This is often something that we say naturally, but in truth, it's something that we take for granted quite a lot. We don't think about it until it actually happens, but often, we don't appreciate others, and that is a problem. Appreciating the good, the actions that others bestow to you, everything, is a key part of leading your own life. To be a good leader, you have to embrace the good, and not focus on the bad.

In the next chapter, we'll dive into that, and why it is imperative that we start to appreciate the good, rather than the bad, in our lives. But for now, let's look at the good, the various things that are happening that are actually important, and why it is important to appreciate the good.

To put it simply, if we appreciate the good things, more good things will come to us. For example, if you focus on the job that you have, how good it is, how you're changing your life, and even the small steps you've taken towards your goal, you'll realize that things are going pretty solid in your life. However, if you focus on how much of a problem your job is, how overwhelming your goals are, focusing on all the negative problems that are there, you're going to breed negativity. Negativity begets negativity, and the same with positive.

You ever wonder why some people just totally rock their jobs, do well, and often don't have problems? It's because, simply, that they aren't letting the negativity take over. They're being the positive influences that they want to be, and in general are happy.

So now that you know why we should be positive, and appreciate the good in the world, how in the world do you do it? What are the best ways to lead your own life, on the road to positivity and happiness? Well, you're about to find out.

Expressing Gratitude

When was the last time you truly appreciated someone or something? Think about it. You probably will think about this question and realize that you haven't truly appreciated something in a long time. Building up gratitude is really the best step to appreciating the good in life. Being mindful of this is important too.

There are a few things that you can start with. First, whenever someone does something for you, or you get help, thank them for it. What you should do, is be really mindful of how you say thank you. Do you mean it? Actually, work to mean the thank-yous that you dole out to others. You'll begin to realize over time that you actually haven't really truly thanked someone for it. If you do this, you'll realize over time that you haven't done it enough, so you'll get into the mindset of doing it more.

Next, you should try to journal a few things that you're thankful and appreciate every single day. This can be anything from the opportunities that you're given, to even appreciating the fact that you're alive. Expressing gratitude towards this, appreciating the good that you've been given, all of this, is really helpful, and it can make everything a lot easier for you as well. Actually, really look at your life and spot what you appreciate, write it down, and really dwell on it. Appreciating what you have will allow you to be the change that you want to be, and you'll start to see that you are doing a lot of good for others.

The last thing to do, is to start to be more mindful. Mindfulness is something that will benefit everyone, whether it be in terms of bettering yourself, others, or the like. If you actually walk through your life, see what you're doing, become more mindful of what you're engaging in, including actions that affect your goals, you'll begin to realize that you're doing a lot of good for yourself, and you'll appreciate these efforts more.

Even something as small as actually going through to the very end and seeing what you're doing with something, paying attention to the drive that you take every day, or even how you compose yourself, can change you, and you'll begin to realize the difference all of this makes within you, and even how it will affect your life.

Becoming more mindful of the positive influences, expressing your gratitude, and the like, will change you, and it will help you become a much stronger person now, and in the future.

Engaging in the Positive Influences

Being positive isn't just being mindful of your actions, it's engaging in the positive efforts that will help you as well.

For example, let's say that you want to lead your life by losing weight, being healthy, and the like. What you should do, is each time you do the right thing, give yourself a pat on the back. Be happy that you're taking life by the horns, trying to better yourself, and doing it well. All too often, whenever we're trying to accomplish a goal, we focus on the things we've done wrong, or even some of the obstacles that come about. Yes, obstacles are there to challenge us, to really pull us forward, but let's be real, for some of us, it can be quite trying to focus on that, not really focusing on the good, the positive influences, and the like that have really helped you propel yourself forward.

When it comes to your actions, always work your goals towards a positive ending. All too often, we have these goals in life that might seem fine, but at the end of it, it actually hurts us, making life a whole lot harder. But, for many of us, if we do work towards putting our fingers into the positivity baskets and actions, we'll be able to make a better decision in life.

It also means that we should learn to appreciate the positive efforts that are put forward. If we actually work towards doing the right thing, having the positive influences nearby to help us, and in general are happy, we'll be a lot better off.

Sometimes, when it comes to setting goals and the like, we tend to set them, but continue to engage in the actions that won't really help us. In order to really appreciate the good in the world, actually working to express ourselves in a better manner, you need to start to look at the negative actions that you're doing, learn that they are negative, and start to do away with them. If you've got negative friends and family, start to move a bit away from them. Still try to appreciate when they help, but you definitely should start to work towards these positive influences.

What this means as well, is that realize that there is good in everything, you should look for that and start to harness it. Yes, people can be trying, it can be rough when it comes to trying to do the right thing, but by actually working to increase your own happiness and energy output by being a positive influence, you'll be happier. So be the person that you want to be, appreciate the good efforts bestowed to you, and don't focus on the negative things that happen to you.

How Positivity Affects Your Goals

For those that wonder just what this might mean for your goals, simply put, it will change them.

Have you ever seen someone that says that they want to accomplish this goal, but in general are always so negative about everything in life? Chances are, they're focusing way too much on the negative, and not appreciating the good that they have. Remember, Rome wasn't built in a day, so your goals won't magically come to fruition the second you say them. It takes hard work, dedication, and a bit of time. It's important to remember that you need to appreciate what you've been given, stay humble, and work towards your goals.

Now, let's take a moment to imagine what it would be like if we focused only on the good, on the positive influences that we've had, on the good things that happen. Appreciating the good in life and focusing on that could change us. It could make our goals seem more realistic, happier, and overall just way better as a result. We'll feel like we're actually getting somewhere, and each little step, each day that we go through working on this, and all of the positive influences, can help you change this.

But, if our minds are only focused on the negativity, on the problems, on the obstacles that are there, all of that, it'll make us feel a whole lot worse as a result. We won't feel happy. We truly won't. We'll continue to only wallow in misery. If we don't appreciate the progress that we're making, instead only focusing on the negative influences that have come forward, on the problems that we're facing, on how hard it is to accomplish this, then guess what, it'll continue to be rough for everyone, not easy, and overall quite a bit of work. It'll definitely make a difference if we changed our thoughts, our mindset, and began to think in a positive manner.

So what is the best course of action? The best thing to do is to appreciate it all. Appreciate the goals that you're accomplishing, how much you've changed, and if you don't realize that you've changed, sit down, look at yourself, and actually realize this. You'd be surprised at how much of a difference this will make, and how much better you'll feel as a result of this. Work towards leading your life in the direction that you want it to go into, and work towards better success.

By doing this, you'll be able to become the best person that you can be. The person that you hope to become, the influence that you wish to be. Be the best person that you know you can be, and work to appreciate the good. Start to thank others, and appreciate what others do for you, and focus on the good things rather than the bad. I can assure you, it'll make the struggle less of a struggle, and you'll feel much better as well.

Chapter 10: How to Become Less Pessimistic

Pessimism is something that we all seem to breed within ourselves. Pessimism is the way of thinking where you believe everything is bad, that there isn't any good in the world, and really just looking at everything from a negative outlook. But, doing that actually can stifle your means to being a great leader and achieving your goals. How do you become less pessimistic then, allowing you to lead your life in a better manner? Well, you're about to find out.

It's rough out there. It's hard to not always think negatively. But as said before, negativity breeds negativity. For many people, becoming less pessimistic is way easier said than done. Some of us were made pessimistic due to life events, others are pessimistic from the moment that we're born. Whatever the case may be, it can be quite hard to turn off that switch that will make you less pessimistic, but if you're able to do so, it can change your life.

Your inner critic

Now, one of the biggest culprits to being the leader that you want to be, is your own inner critic. This is that inner voice that is kind of like a coach that tells you to go away from your goals. This is a means to deter you in order to help you feel "safe" by being on the defensive instead of trying to change yourself. It's mostly the idea of keeping the status quo and only staying in your old identity. This little voice in your head will tell you that you're not doing the right thing because you're not being the old you. It tries to reinforce the idea that the old identity that you grew up with is the one you should be following. It will try to deter you and try to undermine your own personal desires. It will say that you're not capable of doing what you want, warning you about taking chances and trying something new. It will try to admonish by saying that if you do go for what you feel is right for your life, you're setting yourself up for a humiliating failure.

Have you ever had that? It's really the anti-self, which in essence is the person that's against what you truly want in life. It's a destructive point of view that is something that we all have early on in life and comes with us for the ride. This is the voice that is self-critical, cynical towards others, makes you hate yourself, gives you that feeling of anxiety and suspicion, and in the end, is really destructive not only to you, but to others as well. Your real self, looking at it in contrast, is made up of what you want in life. It is what your goals will want to push forward. Pessimism is actually born from the anti-self trying to push these ideas forward onto the self that you have, and it's the reason why you might view life through a critical and cynical eye.

Our brains are focused on the dangerous events that happen in life. Because of this, childhood events will sit there and still cause trouble later on in life, and it actually can end up leading a stronger impression on us than the positive ones that we might have. Sometimes, we tend to have moments where we "lose it" and that can be scary for those around us, and if that ever happened to you as a kid, it can ultimately be a scary event. If you've ever had a moment like that as a kid, it can create a huge emotional impact on you, and for children, the internalized and destructive feelings that caretakers have during moments of stress are the reason why children can often be critical of various elements later on.

The lives of others do influence this, and sometimes, when you sit back and differentiate this, you often notice that these voices can get worse for you. Have you ever felt anxious when you work towards achieving a goal, noticing that critical thoughts are in the way and they're trying to undermine you, such as in the way of procrastinating, saying that it won't work for you, and in general, creates a huge problem? That is the negative thoughts that you've accumulated over time, and it is why pessimism forms in people.

So, if you do have this happen to you, and you still want to change your life, the simple answer, is to say to your inner critic that you don't have time for that. The second you start to feel like all hope is lost, that you're attacking yourself, and you aren't trying to better yourself, stop that and recognize it immediately. Don't even try to argue with it, but instead remind yourself that these inner thoughts are never appropriate to have towards yourself. Realize that you're being pessimistic, and start on the path towards something this negative thinking. Remember though, that these voices are very subtle, and they try to attack you when you're weak. They can sound friendly to you, and they can try to tempt you, saying that you shouldn't work on that goal today, to go exercise, or take the reins on your life, instead, you should try to realize for yourself that you do have a chance to better yourself, you can get the most out of your life, and in general, you can be happy. Be the person that you want to be, work towards the future that you so desire, and do take the time to ensure that you really have the life that you want, and don't let this negativity start to flood over into the rest of the other aspects of your life.

The company you keep

The people that you hang around play a huge part in this. For many of us, sometimes the reason why we're so pessimistic and very stuck in the negative thoughts that we have, is because we are trying to work towards a goal with the wrong people in our life.

In life, there are those that look through it with the glass half full, and those that think it's half empty. There are those that feel like they can still win the battle, and those that feel like it's already over. There are those that love to partake in doom and gloom, and having that around all the time will only make you feel even worse.

That is why you should first and foremost, always look at the company that you keep, especially if they are related to your goals. These people that are always pessimistic, will start to invade your thoughts, and they will make it so hard for you to actually try to work on your goals, being the leader that you already are. These are the people that, when you tell them you've accomplished something, they will come at you and say that it's not worth it, that it's really not super great, and these people do make the element of even trying to work towards a brighter future super hard. Being a better leader includes smiting some of those negative influences, and also looking at what you're doing in your life.

You want to surround yourself with people that will lift you up when you fall. Having people around as part of your team, or even people to help you continue along the way will make the journey much easier. Some might believe that it's better to go alone, but that isn't the case. The truth is, there are some benefits to going alone, but if you really want to be successful, you got to have those that will support you. If getting towards your goals is the key part here, you should try to do this with people that will support you in the best ways possible. Do it with those that are a lot about you, that do love you, that want to be by your side.

Actually, try to find those that will help to push you through this, and often, for many of us, connecting to the cause and having something worth fighting for will knock out that negative voice.

In contrast, having those that are always negative, not going towards their goals, always down about everything, will make you feel bad. It's as simple as that, and it's magical what will happen the second you take charge and start to be around people who aren't always filled with the doom and gloom of life. Yes, it's hard out there, but you don't need to be around people that will only make the journey harder. Go towards people that will actually try to better you, that care enough about you to make a difference, and be around those that care enough to make sure that you're doing okay, and that you're happy. Your future does depend on this, and you should try your hardest to make it the best that it can be.

Limiting social media

Social media is one of the best tools out there for you, but also one of the worst tools out there for you. This ties into the company that you keep. With recent events, such as political issues, social issues, and the like, you probably can't go anywhere without your social media spewing out some sort of information that will make you feel like garbage. The thing is, social media has given people a chance to express themselves, which is great and all, but the problem is, it also causes people to deal with the onslaught of problems that come with the exposure to these people. This can mean that you see stories that bring you down, lots of problems that seem to only get worse as you continue to read, and in general it can be super negative.

Plus, it's distracting. Have you ever spent a long time on social media, only to stop and realize you've wasted hours there? It's because it's a distraction tool, something that you seem to spend a lot of time on, but you don't get a whole lot of good form it.

So, should you abandon all social media, go live off the grid, and just ignore everyone? Not necessarily, but you can limit it, and change it. Limiting does include staying away from the negative influences there that might cause issues, but it also involves trying to filter out the negative stuff. On Facebook, there is a purity checker that can help with this, and some other social media sites have this too. Use it to your advantage, for it can help.

But not only that, start to make the place a positive influence on you. Try to reblog art, use it as a way to read inspirational stories and be in groups that are likeminded to you. You should look for groups related to your goal, connect with them, and start to talk to them. They can really help with this, since often, there are those that have the stories there, and reading them can make you not only feel better about this, but it can deepen the connection that you have with the journey that you're undertaking, and also, it will help you to push yourself forward into a better situation. Sometimes, leading our own life does involve trying to limit the negativity that comes with various aspects of social media, and instead, working on trying to become stronger as a result from all that you've read.

Being pessimistic won't really get you anywhere. It will cause you to have a negative viewpoint, and it is partially the reason why many people want to be leaders, but they don't have a chance to. Recognize this, and start to do something about this, and over time, you'll become a better leader as well.

Chapter 11: How to Propel Yourself Forward to a Better life

Sometimes, it's getting started that is the real struggle. If you feel like you're just dragging yourself through life, trying desperately to get the party started, the ball rolling, or whatever it might be, then it's time that you start to work on leading your own life, pushing yourself forward, and actually working to become the leader that you want to be. But, how in the world do you do this? Well, you're about to find out.

Changing your routine

Do you ever feel like you're really just struggling to get started because of your daily routine? This is often the first culprit that you look into when it comes to changing your life. Look at the routine you've put forward. Is a generic one? Do you struggle to even get out of bed most days? Well, changing this can help get you the push that you need to be your own leader.

A leader takes control and does what they want, has a specific goal that's put forward. Falling into the tedium of daily existence is how being a leader gets smote, and this can be something as simple as not getting up when your alarm tells you to. With being a leader, it involves taking control and the initiative, which can be hard, but if you start to do little bits and pieces of this each and every single day, you'll be able to make a difference.

Let's take getting out of bed. If you're the type of person that tries to sleep through twenty alarms, what you should do, is wake up to the first one, and have that as a goal. Even if it means clenching your fists as you get up, regretting all of your life choices as you do this, it'll become easier with time. Start to become the controller of your own life, and you should start by doing this in small increments.

Maybe get up five minutes earlier, then ten, and then fifteen. If that is what you can accomplish, start with that. This will demonstrate to you as a person, that it is possible to be a leader.

For some of us, we need that reassurance that we can even be leaders. It's hard you there, especially if you've fallen into the daily trap of always being a follower. However, if you can keep the goal at the helm, working towards that, and doing what you know is right, then you'll be able to become the best leader that you can be. It starts off with something small, since this will prove to you that being a leader is doable in your life, and it can make a huge difference in how your functionality works later on.

Keeping goals at the forefront

Goals are what will make you the best leader that you can be. However, when trying to lead by accomplishing your goals, there is that occasion where the goals tend to just up and disappear. This is why people will say that they wish they "finished projects" or have these dreams that they ended up never fulfilling. It's because they didn't take the time to put their goals at the forefront, and to keep their eyes on the prize. As a leader of your own life, you should have the goals relevant to your own life at the helm. Just like in a business, the goals related to the overall success must be the driving force.

You should take a moment to look over your goals that you've already put down, but from there, make sure they're constantly in our mind. Keep the bigger picture, the end result, the goal that you're striving to achieve, at the top of it all. It doesn't matter if you have it written down in a notebook that you use every single day, or taped to your fridge, just have the goal there.

Continue to remind yourself of the goal. Humans are sometimes bad with this, since often we act as if we have our minds open to a whole lot of other issues, thinking about everything, and for many of us, this is how many times we forget about various issues that we have. However, by making sure that you remember your goals, by keeping a daily reminder, and working on them each day, you'll definitely become the leader of your own life.

And if you start to notice that the goal is slipping away, that you're not thinking about it nearly as much, put yourself back in the driver's seat, and work towards this. It shouldn't be some sort of painful affair to get this done. In fact, it should be fun for you to do. Get your goals all nicely lined up, neatly put together into little baskets, and you'll begin to realize the impact that this has on it. Even if you're not a fan of doing it this way, actually start to work on trying to remember your goals, and do it easily.

By remembering goals, it'll be like that constant little voice in your head, gently reminding you that you have aspirations, that you have desires in your life that you want to accomplish. Many times, the reason why we're not happy, is because those goals of the past, those little aspirations that we had, are long-gone. But don't let your dreams fall away, like they're something that goes away with time. That isn't how this works. Goals should always be worked on, regardless of who you are, and the state of your life. Even if it is a little bit, it goes a long way with time. Work on our personal goals, try to achieve them, and from there, you should start to notice the difference that you make in your own life, the way your life seems to run, and the difference in your personal leadership.

Work to challenge yourself

This kind of goes with the earlier point on differentiating your routine. When it comes to both getting into the spirit of being a leader, and also achieving your goals, you gotta give yourself a challenge. The biggest problem that many people face, is the fact that they're not being challenged enough in life. When you're bored, some small problems become huge problems, and the actual problems are kind of sitting there behind the curtain and not being taken care of. When it comes to your goals, sure the little ones that are achievable are definitely worth mentioning, but it's important to express yourself efficiently, to challenge yourself to the point where actually going for your goals is fun, and not some sort of burden that will make it harder on you.

This can be something as simple as maybe trying to beat the quota that you had last week in your business. This can be trying to go to the gym three times a week versus once, and recording your progress. Maybe it's running thirty minutes on the treadmill rather than ten. Whatever it might be, you need to figure out the best means to challenge yourself, and the best ways to feel like you're really putting up a fight.

This doesn't have to take a lot either. You can look at the goals that you have, choose what you want to work on, and put the bar set at one level. When you achieve that, put it slightly higher. Now, when you do try to lead your life, don't make the expectations so high that you'll never reach them. Don't make it so that you're leading a ship that will never make it to the destination. Remember, you've got to be realistic with this, and you need to do what you feel is right.

Each day, make sure that you've got that challenge put in. Greet each day with a happy tone, but also look with the mindset of "what can I do to challenge myself today?" all too often, for many people, they tend to think "well, what will I get through today?" and not really manage to achieve anything. If you want to sit in the realm of the status quo, and if you want to continue to be a follower, then fine, take the easy way out and don't challenge yourself. But if you want to see what you can do, then try to become the best person that you can be through the art of the challenge. Greet each day with the idea that you'll get more done than the day before, and with the idea that you'll put yourself through the ringer without any worry. If you can manage to think like that, and with the idea that it's not scary to be successful and leading your own life, then you'll surely make it, no matter what others might say to you.

Dare to Be Different

One thing that you should think about doing is work to be different. This is something that as a leader, you should always be working on, especially in order to propel yourself forward. Remember, we're all different at the core, but with the identity formed courtesy of the place we've grown up, the life we lived, the caretakers that we have had, all of that can play a huge part in that. We tend to act like the characteristics that we've taken in, bringing forth those personalities rather than creating our own. Typically, we tend to live the lives of other people if we do this, rather than actually living our own life. We should make sure that we are working to live our own life and destiny, and differentiate this from the environment that we live in.

Typically, our true identity is down there, and it's affected by the personal experiences that we've had. This can either help or harm up, and we start to cope with our fears. However, from this, we not only adapt ourselves to the environment, we tend to lose sight of the common goal, and often don't really think about what we want in life, or even what we are doing. This means that often, we're really not looking at the person we should be, and not working to be our true form.

What that means for you, is that you should sit down, and make sure you're doing everything that you want to do. Be your own boss, be the one in control, and don't be afraid to try and work through this yourself. This is a very personal thing, because often, sitting there and realizing that you've been living the life of a lie can be quite stimulating. There are many of us who, because of societal situations, and because of the way things are, we tend to think that our lives are unfulfilling, and we tend to get tired of life. But, maybe it's because of the fact that you're not doing what you truly love

What you should do, is really look at who you are, the job that you're working, the life that you're living, and really look into if you're doing what you love, or if it's just your mind playing tricks on you. You'd be surprised at how many of us tend to think we're doing the right thing, but then in truth, we're actually not. It can be quite the rude awakening, and it can be a bit shocking, but if you do look at this through a realistic sense, start to write down what you want, and work towards your goals, you can undo all of that. If you've been forced into a career that you hate, a life that you don't like, and in general feel empty a lot of the time, sometimes it's because you're afraid to differentiate, afraid to be yourself, but remember, what has being a follower ever gotten anyone? Being a leader is where you should be focusing, and the type of life you should be living.

Work on your personal power

Personal power is what you have, and often, it can be hard to find. Typically, those that find it do a bit of digging within themselves, harnessing it after they realize they've been the self-criticizers that they've been all their life. This can be a bit shocking, but it is your own personal strength, competence, and confidence that many people seem to get throughout the course of their development. This is who you really are, and it is what you should always be working towards.

It's a self-assertion that does show a sort of natural need to love, to be successful, to have the satisfaction and the meaning that you so desire in life. It is the power to create the dreams that you want to have, and it is who you really are. You should recognize this whenever you start to move towards your goals. Whenever you're working on a goal that works for you, and when you start to realize you are a born leader, you'll start to realize that you feel stronger. It's a common action to see your own strength when you do what's right for you, and what's best for you.

This can also be something as small as actively trying to work on bettering yourself. Start to meditate, really look into yourself, and figure out who you really are. Sometimes connecting with the real self that you are, the one that isn't tired and overworked from not doing what it wants to, but the rejuvenated sort of being that you truly are, can be a great thing, and it can be quite amazing when you do realize this. If you feel like you're still missing something, start to look at the personal power.

It is a state of mind that we can develop, one that we can use by getting in touch with ourselves, getting out of bed and taking control, and working to ignore the criticism that we have going on. Sometimes the biggest push forward is realizing just how strong we are, and how we can propel our lives, and you can realize this through the use of understanding and living through the idea of making sure that you have control over who you are as a person, and who you are in life.

When it comes to even getting the energy to get started, it can be hard for many of us, but this chapter talked a bit about how you can get started with being your own leader today. At the end of the day, it does all come down to the goals that you have, and if you're working on them. By actively working on yourself, and working on the future that you so care to uphold, you'll become even stronger than you've ever imagined, bigger and better than before, and in general, you'll feel the power from your own decisions, and from the leadership that you've decided to take on.

Chapter 12: Learning from Mistakes and Pushing Forward

Mistakes are a part of life. They are something that you sometimes have to go through, something that isn't quite fun to deal with. But, did you know that mistakes are a huge part of learning lessons? A huge part of leadership involves this, because all too often, we tend to not humble ourselves down and admit that we've made mistakes. This chapter will go over how mistakes are a part of leadership, and how learning from them is important.

Everyone makes mistakes

For many of us, making mistakes is often something that you don't want to admit to yourself. You need to realize from this that everyone does make mistakes, and if you do manage to take responsibility for it, you'll be able to understand and learn from it. The good thing about this, is that you don't have to publicly tell the world you've made a mistake. You should at least admit to yourself that you have, and don't blame others for the actions that you take.

This is counter to many of the assumptions that are out there. For many of us, we're always taught that we should feel guilty every time that we mess up, that making mistakes is utter failure, and you should never make them. It sets us all up to be these kinds of crazy perfectionists, since often, this is what happens when you give up on your goals after a mistake is made.

For many that try to be leaders in their own life, this is the first thing that need to learn. You need to learn that mistakes will be made. None of us are perfect. That's the reality of the situation. You're not perfect, and you never will be perfect. That's what many people need to learn when trying to lead a better life, and to not give up on their goals.

What is missing in many of our lives is the idea that the higher and more challenging the goal is, the higher chance and higher frequency of setbacks and difficulties. The larger the ambitions are, the more you'll need to really on the ability to make sure that you do take a look at what you're doing, realize that mistakes will be made, and learn to overcome these feelings.

You're going to make mistakes. It is implied in our minds, and in society as well, that if you make a mistake, you fail, but it actually is something that you need to realize is a part of life. You might seem to be someone that has always been perfect, and someone who has never made mistakes, but often, you lose our self-identity with this obsession with this. You're going to lose a lot of ground if you don't realize that making mistakes will help you learn. We've been indoctrinated to believe that if we make a mistake, we're nothing, but oftentimes, the only way to truly be the person that you want to be is by making mistakes, learning how the world works, and so on and so forth. Think about it, our lives are often pushed into this mindset that we need to basically parrot off these facts, never step you of bounds, and in general never really be courageous, compassionate, or even creative in our own lives. We have to follow the status quo in order to get anywhere, which is so far from the truth it's not funny. In essence, you need to realize that you have to make mistakes, take a few risks, and try to become a better person from these mistakes.

Everyone does make mistakes and it's important to know you're not going to be the odd person out because of it. You need to get it through our head that simply put, everyone makes mistakes. You need to be smart about it, humble yourself, and learn to admit it.

Why Complaining Won't Get You Anywhere

The problem with this, is that most of us suffer from not being able to admit that we've made mistakes, and instead dwell on it, end up worrying about it, or in general complain about it. However, that won't enrich you, won't allow you to learn, and in general is a dangerous mindset. Why is that though? Well, let's dive deeper into this.

Let's say that you make a mistake. You do it, you hate yourself, whatever. When you do this, you immediately form regret, or start to loathe what you did. Regret is a normal human emotion, and a way to respond to something. However, when you regret a decision, it holds it in place, and you'll come back to it later on. If you dwell on mistakes, you'll start to feel your self-confidence diminish, along with your creativity. You might start to notice that you're really not doing a whole lot. Sometimes, and often in many of us and probably in your mind right now, we can trigger the need to be perfect, and procrastinate, which in turn creates stress on yourself, along with fear, worry, and even frustration. Do you want to live like that? Probably not, and if you do, you should probably take a look at what is going on. You should realize that mistakes are a means to transform your life, and you'll notice that it is something that we've all got wrong.

Most people dwell on mistakes because of the past, and its why people act as if mistakes are terrible and unwanted. Some might have a different experience, but often mistakes aren't viewed as good, but rather as something terrible and shouldn't be made, which is why you probably struggle with self-expression today.

Now, let's take those that complain about their mistakes, the things they've done in the past, the whole nine yards. Have you ever complained about something that you did a long time ago, thinking that the mistake is the sole reason why your life is one way or another? Chances are, if you don't realize that you have to stop complaining about what you've done, and instead learn from your mistakes, you'll never get better. You've got to learn, even though it might be rough.

Admitting that you screwed up does take a lot of courage. If you don't, you won't ever become braver about trying new things, you won't take risks, and most of all, you won't take responsibility. This is why with many people, the mindset of "everyone else is to blame and not me" is often a huge part of this, and it is something that you need to realize for yourself. It might be a bit of a shocker to realize, but if you do admit your mistakes, stop complaining and dwelling on them, you'll be a whole lot happier.

Think about it in this regard. You've probably seen either a parent or a grandparent say that they wish they did things differently, that they wish they never got into that business deal, whatever it might be. If you're someone that feels this way, chances are, you're not taking responsibility for it, and instead, you needed to realize that you are the one leading our own life, and you're the one that needs to realize that this isn't what you should be doing, but instead, you need to grab life by the horns, admit that you messed up, and start to learn from it.

Learning Lessons from Mistakes

When learning, you've got four types of mistakes. Stupid ones, just careless mistakes, simple mistakes which are avoidable but your decisions made it inevitable. For example, maybe running out of food because you didn't anticipate the crowd coming in. Involved are mistakes that you need to actually actively work on to prevent, such as arriving late to work or eating bad food every single day. Complex mistakes are often those that have complex reasons for them happening, and something you've got to work on next time, such as a failing relationship or maybe a business decision with bad results.

Now, there are different ways to learn from these mistakes. Really, it's mostly going through and recognizing the problem, and avoiding similar mistakes. In the case of maybe stubbing our toe, watch out for maybe that toy on the floor, or pick up after yourself. If you have a party and you run out of food, make sure to get a real RSVP from everyone before the next one. It's really as simple as that. Now, it's important to remember that mistakes that you make do define you, but it also means that these are the ones that you best learn from. With mistakes that are stupid, you should really just try to avoid them. You should try to also challenge yourself too. If you're getting hung up on missing your favorite tv show, you've got to figure out something bigger. Give yourself a bigger goal.

For those that are involved, you've got to make big changes to avoid these. These are the ones that we make via habit, such as maybe eating too much fast food, or sugar all the time. Change is hard to begin in one's life, which is why these mistakes are happening again and again, and we need to make the changes from this.

Now, with involved mistakes, some feel like they need to realize they have to make a change first. You should recognize that things are going south, and once you realize that, maybe write down what you can do. Set up a schedule, create a goal, work to maintain it. All of these things will help you actively see the mistakes. One big hurdle with this however, is that sometimes, there might be the situation that nothing is wrong, that you don't need to worry about this, however, you should take a moment to realize that you've made the commitments to do this, and you need to make a change. You should sit there and try to take responsibility for this, and don't try to place the blame on others. This is complicated for most, but it is necessary in order to be the successful person that you so desire to be.

For very complex mistakes, you need to first and foremost is to actually get different perspectives on the situation. For example, if you feel like you totally screwed up a relationship, you should talk to someone about what happened, and get their perspective on the situation. You can talk to those associated with the mistake, or even just someone who is impartial to the whole debacle. Let them tell you what they think, and you should then take an honest look at what happened. Look at the sequence of events, what had been going on, and from there, you should realize what had gone on.

For example, if your car got totaled, look at what the signs of it failing would've been. Did you get the brakes checked? Were you distracted? You should definitely consider this as well. Listen to others, since they have different perspectives of the situation, and you should definitely have an unbiased viewpoint on all of this together. You need to look at everything, see where you went wrong, and actually investigate the whole mistake. Do what you feel is best by looking backwards, working backwards, and seeing exactly where you need to make changes. From there, write them down, and then do these changes. It will help you with making mistakes.

Remember, everyone needs to make mistakes. That's the only way that we grow. But you want to learn from the mistakes that you've made. The four kinds of mistakes are listed here, and it's important that as a person, you recognize these in order to avoid them in the future.

How to take your Faults and make Them your Strengths

Now that you know how to learn from mistakes, there are a few guidelines that will help you get the most out of this. It is important to realize that you need to realize a few points for everything to work out.

The first, is you gotta take responsibility for your mistakes. This is how you learn. Don't think that making mistakes means you are a mistake. You can't change them when they happen, and you aren't a failure, but you need to respond to them better.

Start to work to improve yourself. See where you can improve, and see what information needs to be learned to avoid mistakes.

When it comes to various mistakes, you have to learn why it happened and what factors are there, and what the sequences of the smaller mistakes lead to bigger ones. You should work to consider all alternatives, and work to make changes, even if they are difficult. Recognize that mistakes are hard for you, and it can be difficult to realize, but it is worth it.

You should also assess your behavior. Do learn to understand how you got into that mess, and realize that there are a few ways to help change the situation.

Also, don't think that this one situation is the only one. There are others, so realize that each experience is different.

Making mistakes is a part of life. It stinks, but you have to realize that they exist. If you can realize that you do make mistakes, you'll have a much better experience, and overall, a much better time in the future.

Conclusion

Being the leader of your own life is hard work, but this book told you how to do it. The biggest part of this, isn't the fact that you are going to lead, but it is the decision to rightfully lead something like this. Let's face it, it's not easy. It won't be, and it never will be, but if you go into it with the mindset that you can work hard, dedicate yourself to the cause, and learn from the mistakes of the past, you'll feel way better as a result of this. And, you'll learn to control your life in the best of ways as well.

That's the next step. Get started with becoming the leader of your own life. It shouldn't take much to begin, but rather, it's just getting started. The beginning is really the hardest part, but if you take the time to seriously look at yourself, see the difference that you can make, and then do something about it, you'll see the difference almost immediately. Get the support that you need as well, for that will help spiral you to new heights.

Most of all, have fun with this. Being a leader shouldn't be hard work. It shouldn't be an obstacle that's impossible for you to overcome. What it should be, is a decision, one that you rightfully make yourself, and you'll be able to become the dealer of your own fate, the person that makes yourself happy, and most of all, you'll be able to reap the benefits of doing this immediately. So, do it. Get started, and you'll never be the same again. Be the change what you want to be, the leader that you know you can be, and start doing this today.

www.ingramcontent.com/pod-product-compliance
Lightning Source LLC
Chambersburg PA
CBHW070315230526
45470CB00002B/887